THE BARTENDER'S GUIDE TO GIN

THE BARTENDER'S GUIDE TO GIN

Classic and modern-day cocktails for gin lovers

CONTENTS

A brief

HISTORY of GIN

The gin we know today tells a story that spans many centuries. From its most humble beginnings as a drink of the poor and destitute to its association as the drink of privilege and royalty, gin has quite a colourful tale to tell.

Distillation, of which gin is just one product, is an ancient art – the first stills were filled by Arabic alchemists in the Far East as early as the 1st century when the Roman Empire was in full swing and Christianity was in its formative years. These early scientists spent decades distilling all manner of elixirs, gleaning knowledge from other specialists of the time, such as the Greeks.

By the 12th century the knowledge had been absorbed into Europe and was being used by Benedictine monks in Salerno, Italy. At this point, spirit was used for medical and scientific

reasons, in order to preserve the rare and precious ingredients used in medicine. These early distillations of alcoholic spirit would have tasted truly awful, due to the primitive distillation process.

Thanks to the Benedictine monks, distillation began to spread gradually through other monasteries in Europe. The process was still crude, but over the centuries it was refined by Europe's scientific minds. By the 1600s, distillation was widely used and the use of grain- and grape-based spirits was commercialized into liquors such as Chartreuse, Armagnac and gin's forerunner, genever.

Genever is a grain-based spirit made in pot stills, (much like whiskey) flavoured with Juniper and in some cases aged in oak casks. The name 'genever' is derived from the Dutch word for Juniper and is pronounced *yey-nih-ver*. It is still made in some of the oldest distilleries in the world, such as Amsterdam's Bols Distillery, which dates back to 1575. Nowadays Genever isn't so well known outside the Low Countries and specialist drinks circles, but without it we would not have gin as we know it.

Gin became hugely popular throughout the 1600s. The Thirty Years' War, which raged across Europe from 1618–1648, made other spirits much harder to acquire, while the Dutch East India Trading Company (known as the VOC) was actively developing overseas markets. Genever had also become a staple of the Dutch military and, in turn, of English soldiers who had been sent by Queen Elizabeth I to fight alongside them. The Thirty Years' War was one of Europe's bloodiest wars, but we do have it to thank for the dramatic influx of genever coming across the English Channel.

The taste for gin soon became ingrained in London. In the early 1700s, British distillers keen to emulate the flavour and success of genever started to produce the first English gin. Because there were no strict laws surrounding licensing and production, London hosted a massive boom of spirits. These early English gins were made using various methods and ingredients – some were downright toxic, but they were all made from grain and flavoured with juniper. The period from the early 1700s to the 1750s is the ugliest chapter in gin's history and the source of many of the myths that still surround the spirit. After a series of acts introduced by the Government to control the gin craze, London started to sober up and some iconic gin brands started to emerge.

With the 1800s came the age of the cocktail, and in the 1830s the birth of the 'column still', which was to revolutionize the production of gin, and all spirits. The column enabled a far purer spirit style because of its vastly more efficient distillation mechanics. With a cleaner and purer spirit, producers started to remove the sugar and other additives, which were no longer needed to mask their distillates – and dry gin was born.

Illustration of a gin shop from Charles Dickens' *Sketches by Boz* (1836).

English Gin was now on the up, the hideous gins of the 1700s had gone and fine-quality dry gins began to be appreciated the world over. The drink flourished even during US Prohibition, and having survived two world wars, bounced back and continued to grow into the mid-1950s. Gin then took a back seat, making way for vodka, but from the noughties onwards we have seen a true renaissance, and an explosion of gins being produced around the world.

FROM GRAIN *to* GLASS

In its simplest form, gin is a pure spirit that has been flavoured with juniper and other botanicals. A spirit is generally made using either pot or column stills and is the product of distilling an alcoholic solution that is usually made from grapes or grains.

The majority of gins start life as a neutral grain spirit (NGS). This spirit is the product of column distillation, a technique that has been practised since the mid-1800s. This has revolutionised the production of spirits and is used on a mammoth scale in huge distilleries, some of which are capable of producing in excess of 100-million litres/26-million gallons of pure alcohol per annum.

These distilleries are essential to the whole spirits industry, despite being a far cry from the shiny copper stills used in the final stages of the original process of gin-making. To understand NGS and how it is used to make gin, you first need to have an understanding of exactly how alcohol is made.

All alcoholic drinks are the product of a serendipitous relationship between yeast and sugar. Yeast is a single-celled organism and a fungus that, given the right conditions, can transform the fermentable sugars in a sugary liquid into alcohol. The origin of the base liquid will determine the type of beverage being made, so grape juice makes wine, apple juice makes cider, and malt-based liquids make beer.

The art of fermentation has been practised for thousands of years and has now evolved into the many alcoholic beverages we see today.

The spirit used to make the vast majority of English gins is made from grain and distilled using column stills. The grain is milled, mashed with hot water and fermented with yeast to create what the spirits industry call 'wash'. The distillation of spirits works under the basic principle that alcohol has a lower boiling temperature than water. As heat is applied to the still and the temperature rises, the alcohol will begin to separate from the wash and rise up the still as a vapour; it is then collected and condensed back into a liquid, creating the spirit. Column stills are incredibly efficient and, unlike other types of still, can produce an immaculate distillate of incredibly high strength, removing nearly all the impurities along the way. This makes it perfect for making gin.

Unlike malt whisky or Cognac distilleries, many gin distillers tend not to start with the raw materials and fermentation, instead buying NGS and redistilling, rectifying and tweaking it to meet their requirements. This has been encouraged by EU laws on the production of Dry and London gins, dictating that a neutral spirit of no less than 96% alcohol by volume (ABV) must be used as the base spirit for distilled and London/Dry gin. Achieving these strengths with more traditional distilling set-ups can be difficult. The resulting base spirit is then combined with botanicals to give the flavour.

Distillers use various methods, equipment and types of still to infuse and entwine their botanicals into their spirit. The quantities and combinations of botanicals used, along with the infusion methods and equipment used, dictate the gin's style and flavour.

The two most common methods are the 'steep and boil' method and the 'vapour infusion'

method. Steep and boil, as the name suggests, involves steeping the botanicals in the base spirit, which has been cut down to roughly 50–60% abv. Some producers leave the botanicals for a couple of days, others for just a few hours. The next step involves distilling the spirit once again, which finishes the infusion of the botanicals into the spirit.

A gin bottling plant.

For vapour-infused gins, the botanicals are suspended in a basket, usually in the neck of the still – the spirit vapour collects the oils and flavours as it is forced through the basket. Once the vapour has cooled and condensed, a flavourful gin emerges.

There are other methods used, but the goal is always to infuse the botanicals into the spirit. Regardless of precise distillation and infusion methods, all gins will finally be cut down with water to a bottling strength, in most cases 37.5% abv. This is the legal minimum, but less water can be used, resulting in a much stronger release.

BOTANICALS

Botanicals are to gin what paint is to a canvas – without them gin would simply be a neutral spirit with no character. Under the watchful eye of a gin distiller, the botanicals will relinquish their precious oils into the spirit, creating a kaleidoscope of flavour.

By far the most important botanical is juniper. It is, by law, the dominant flavour in gin and provides the lion's share of aroma. Its cones, better known as berries, are bold and fragrant with oil-rich seeds, providing the precious compounds that create the gin's signature flavour. The chemical compound alpha-pinene is dominant, contributing pine, rosemary, lavender, heather and camphor flavours, to name just a few. It also contains limonene, which adds citrus flavours. Both of these compounds appear in many of the botanicals used in the making of gin and are found throughout the plant world, designed to deter hungry insects. It just so happens that what insects don't like, gin drinkers do.

Juniper

Juniper is a robust plant which grows all around the world, but in the making of gin it is mainly sourced from Eastern Europe, Tuscany and Morocco. The plant is tricky and time-consuming to harvest as each plant bears both ripe and unripe berries all year round. On top of this, each berry can take three years to mature before finally being ready to pick. This means the berries must be collected by hand, so as not to disturb the ripening berries and the following year's crop. Every year, hundreds of tons of juniper berries will be harvested from the wild, destined to be absorbed within spirit.

Juniper plays its part in the flavour of gin alongside other botanicals, just like the instruments in an orchestra, to create a symphony of flavour. The most common botanicals found in gin, aside from juniper, are coriander seeds, angelica root, orris root, cassia bark, liquorice and citrus peel.

Coriander seeds

Found in Morocco, Bulgaria, Russia and Romania is the second most important botanical, rich in the essential oil linalool – this is spicy and aromatic, lending woody notes and sparkling citrus and floral flavours.

Angelica root

Mainly sourced from Germany and Belgium, angelica root shares two of the key compounds found in juniper: the woody alpha-pinene and the citric lemolene, but the overall punch is much softer. The root acts as a bond, helping to tie the more volatile flavours together in the spirit.

Orris root

Amongst the rarest ingredients used in gin, orris root is often sourced from Florence, Italy. It takes years for the bulbous root to develop in the plant and it then needs to be stored and dried for a further three years. At this stage the root is very hard and needs to be ground into a powder before being used. Its flavour is far less pronounced than juniper and coriander, but it still plays a key role. Like angelica, it helps to fix the more volatile flavour compounds within the spirit. Many gin distillers praise it for its subtlety and perfumed qualities.

Cassia bark

The cassia tree is a member of the cinnamon family and is usually found growing in China, Vietnam and Madagascar. The bark is collected and dried. Like cinnamon, it brings a warming, festive spiciness.

Liquorice root

Found in Indo-China, this hard, fibrous root needs to be ground down before use and helps add sweetness and balance alongside the livelier and punchier botanicals.

Citrus peel

Both lemon and orange have a key role in most gins – the peels are stripped from the fruit, bringing in their signature flavours. Oranges and lemons from Seville, Spain, where the peels are removed by hand and left to dry in the sun, are generally favoured.

These core botanicals are often supplemented by a medley of others, including cardamom, grains of paradise (alligator pepper), ginger, cubeb berries and aniseed. Gin producers will often also seek out locally grown botanicals to add unique supporting flavours – these add terroir and provenance to individual gins.

Some of gin's botanical flavourings.

With so many exotic, flavourful botanicals, infinite combinations and multiple infusion methods, gin looks set to continue on its streamlined path of innovation, diversity and intoxicating flavours.

DEFINITION and STYLES of GIN

Defining gin

The legal definition of gin is of a distilled spirit that obtains its flavour through juniper and other botanicals. These botanical flavourings can influence the spirit before, during and after distillation, depending on the production method used.

Gin is produced globally and legal definitions can vary slightly around the world, but the core principals remain the same. The principals are that gin must be distilled from a neutral spirit base of ethyl alcohol and the dominant flavour must be juniper.

The minimum bottling strength for gin in Europe is 37.5% ABV, whereas in the US the minimum strength is 40% ABV (80% proof). All types of gin made in Europe are bound by the EU Spirit Drink Regulations of 2008, and fall into one of three categories: Gin, Distilled Gin and London Gin.

Gin

This most basic form of gin is made by adding natural or artificial flavours to the neutral base spirit. This type of gin does not need to be redistilled, and approved artificial colourings and sweeteners can be added. This style is cheaper and easier to make and is usually deemed inferior, due to the lack of restrictions surrounding the quantities of the additives used.

Distilled Gin

This type of gin is made by redistilling a neutral base spirit of at least 96% ABV in the company of botanicals. The resulting flavour-infused distillate can be collected at any given strength and can be flavoured and coloured with permitted additives, both natural and artificial.

London Gin

This type of gin is made using a high-grade neutral spirit of at least 96% ABV, which is re-distilled in a traditional still in the presence of the natural flavourings. The resulting distillate must have a minimum strength of 70% ABV. No artificial sweeteners, colourings or flavours can be added.

Within the three categories of Gin, Distilled Gin and London Gin are found the various styles of gin that we see on the shelves.

London Dry and Dry Gins

This type of gin falls into the London Gin category. It made its debut after the invention of the Coffey/column still in the 1830s. This was the birth of the clean, neutral spirit that enabled the creation of a purer gin. With a cleaner base spirit, distillers discovered that they no longer needed to mask the flavours in their distillates with sweeteners and other additives – and so Dry Gin was born. It was originally made solely in London, but is now made across the world, with many Dry Gins coming from the US. Dry Gin is arguably the cleanest and purest style of gin available.

Old Tom Gin

Falling into the Distilled Gin category, Old Tom was the forerunner of London Dry. Prior to the column still, distillers in London were using various types of pot stills, some with very little skill. Without the correct technical expertise, the distillate from these pot stills would have often tasted pretty grim. To combat the unpleasant flavour, other ingredients were added after distillation to mask the taste. Today Old Tom gins, like all gin, is seeing a revival.

It is typically sweeter than dry styles due to the small amounts of added sugar.

Compound Gins

This type of gin falls into the Gin category. Compound Gins are made by mixing the juniper and botanicals with the neutral base spirit. It traces its origins back to the times of Prohibition and illicit spirit production. Despite being generally deemed inferior, advances in compounding have created significantly better Compound Gins. Some gins of this style are now performing very well within the drinks trade and spirit competitions.

Geographically Indicated Gins

This type of gin can fall into any of the three categories mentioned above. Some wines can only be made in specific areas, and this can also be true for gin. Xoriguer from Menorca, Spain, and Vilnius Dzinas from Lithuania have protected geographical status. Plymouth Gin was one of these, but its status expired in 2015.

Barrel-Aged Gins

This gin can fall into any of the three gin categories. Now becoming increasingly popular, Barrel-Aged Gins undergo a period of time maturing in oak casks. The casks have, in most cases, been previously used to store whiskey.

Sloe Gin

Fruit has always been a natural partner to gin and Sloe Gins can be traced back to the earliest English gins. Due to the large amounts of sloes and sugar, sloe gins are technically liqueurs. They are made by steeping large quantities of ripe sloe berries in the gin. They can be bottled at a much lower minimum strength of 25% ABV.

How to
NOSE and TASTE GIN

Understanding gin

Gin is rarely drunk neat. In a quality gin bar, it will almost certainly be served over ice, garnished and presented alongside a bottle of chilled bubbling tonic. Just perfect.

But if you really want to discover the characteristics of a gin, it is worth taking a few moments to nose and taste the spirit neat, and, in the same way as the tasting of all quality and flavoursome spirits, this nosing and tasting process can take a bit of practice.

Tasting strong spirit neat can come as quite a shock to the senses, especially if you are new to the idea, but by following a few key tips, your senses will soon start to get in gear and reveal the sublime flavours that are hiding behind a mask of alcohol.

Nosing

Nosing is a good way of adapting your senses to the strength of the spirit. This is best done with a nosing glass, but can be done with a wine glass.

Take a modest measure of gin at room temperature, hold the glass a short distance away from your nose and begin to nose it. After a few seconds take the glass away and take a few moments to breathe in and out normally. Then bring the glass back, nose it again, breathing in the aromas, and repeat the process.

Do this a few times, taking breaks, and your olfactory senses will start to get used to the strength and, slowly, you will start to unravel the aromas in your gin. After a few minutes it will seem like a different drink. It's all to do with adapting your senses.

Tasting

You need to take time when tasting spirits neat. Those unfamiliar with strong alcohol will instinctively want to swallow the spirit after just a fraction of a second on the palate, in the same way that they might drink beer or wine. When spirits are tasted in this way, however it can lead to an unpleasant bite and a coarse, burning feeling on the throat and senses.

You can avoid this by tasting the spirit in a different way. Visualize a small teaspoon of liquid, roll it onto your tongue, and hold it there. Then roll it around your mouth, coating your tongue, again holding the spirit for a few seconds. This may feel strange at first, but you will get used to strength and start to find flavour. After the first sip, take a few moments and then revisit the glass. Upon tasting the second and third time, the alcohol and prickliness will have subsided and you will start to discover much more character and flavour.

While nosing and tasting, try to think about how the flavours reveal themselves and the texture of the spirit. This more analytical approach to tasting gin can be very rewarding, especially when you are comparing different gins. But where gin really performs is when it is lengthened in the classic G&T or in a cocktail.

Tonic

When adding tonic to gin, start small and build up. A two-to-one ratio is a good place to start. Like adding salt to food, you can always add more but you can't take it away. A good-quality tonic is of critical importance – adding flat, lifeless, cheap tonic to good gin is an abomination to serious mixologists and should be avoided at all costs. A handful of key brands have started to lead the way over the last few years and have become widely available in supermarkets.

Today many flavoured tonics can also be found, some of which work well with specific gins. Alongside new flavoured tonics, signature serves and elaborate garnishes have become common practice in many bars as gin brands are keen to find a unique selling point for their product. Through this, an almost infinite number of serves have emerged, some that work well, and others that don't. Remember it is the gin that should be bringing the character and flavour to your G&T, not a handful of fruit, leaves or seeds.

By far the most important part of tasting any gin, whether neat, with tonic or in a cocktail, is enjoyment. Drink your gin how YOU like it, and don't let anyone tell you otherwise.

GLASSWARE

Presentation is everything in mixology, so it is important to serve a cocktail in the appropriate glass – the size, shape and style all have an impact on the visual perception and enjoyment of the drink. Here are some of the classic glasses that you will need to have in your collection.

Martini glass

The most iconic of all cocktail glasses, the conical martini glass emerged with the art deco movement. The long stem is perfect for chilled drinks as it keeps people's hands from inadvertently warming the cocktail.

Highball glass

Sometimes also known as a Collins glass, these glasses are perfect for serving drinks with a high proportion of mixer to spirit. The highball glass is versatile enough to be a substitute for the similarly shaped, but slightly larger, Collins glass.

Lowball glass

The lowball glass, also known as a rocks or old-fashioned glass, is a short, squat tumbler and is great for serving any spirit on the rocks or for short, mixed cocktails.

Champagne flute

The tall, thin flute's tapered design reduces the champagne's surface area and so helps to keep the fizz in the drink for longer. The flute has now largely replaced the coupe glass for serving champagne and champagne cocktails.

Shot glass

This glass is a home-bar essential and can hold just enough spirit to be drunk in one mouthful. It also has a firm base that can be satisfyingly slammed on a bar top. The shot glass can also stand in for a measure when making cocktails.

Coupette glass

The coupette or Margarita glass, as its second name implies, was designed specifically for serving Margaritas. It is ideal for any frozen, blended drinks.

Coupe glass

A wide-rimmed glass that is good for serving sparkling drinks, this was once the glass of choice for champagne. Legend has it that the glass is modelled on a woman's breast.

Snifter glass

The bowl-shaped snifter glass invites drinkers to cradle the drink in their hands, warming the contents of the glass, so it is good for winter spirits, such as brandy. The aroma of the drink is held in the glass, allowing you to breathe in the drink before sipping.

Hurricane glass

This pear-shaped glass pays homage to the hurricane lamp and was the glass used to create the New Orleans rum-based cocktail, the Hurricane. It's also used for a variety of frozen and blended cocktails.

Sling glass

A variation on the highball glass, this is a design classic that is used to serve the Singapore Sling and the Long Island Ice Tea. The tall body and short stem of this glass make it ideal for chilled drinks.

MIXOLOGY
EQUIPMENT

The equipment you have in your home bar depends on whether you are a cocktail king or queen who likes all the latest gadgets, or whether you are prepared to make do with some basic options. Nowadays, there is no limit to the amount of bar equipment available, but you absolutely don't need lots of kit to make the majority of the drinks in this book. Here is an outline of the essential tools of the trade.

Measures and jiggers

A jigger (see opposite, top) is a bartender's basic measuring tool and is essential for crafting the perfect blend of ingredients. You can get a steel jigger with clear measurement markings so you can easily and accurately pour out measures.

Bar spoon

A proper bar spoon has a small bowl and a long handle that allows you to muddle, mix and stir with ease. Spoons come in a variety of lengths and widths, and a stylish bar spoon is an attractive addition to any bartender's kit.

Shaker

Most contemporary shakers are made from steel as steel doesn't tarnish readily and doesn't conduct heat easily – this is useful with chilled cocktails as the ice cools the cocktail rather than the shaker. Most standard shakers come with a built-in strainer, but if you're using a Boston or Parisian shaker then you'll need to use a separate strainer.

Mixing glass or beaker

Any vessel that holds about 500 ml/1 pint of liquid can be used for mixing drinks. It is good to have a mixing glass with a spout or ridged rim so that you can stop ice from slipping into the glass, but this is not vital as a strainer can be used. Mixing beakers are increasingly popular nowadays, and are usually made of glass or crystal.

Muddler

For mashing up citrus fruit or crushing herbs, you need a muddler. This is a chunky wooden tool with a rounded end and it can also be used to make cracked ice. You can mash fruit or crush herbs with a mortar and pestle, but the advantage of a muddler is that it can be used directly in the mixing glass.

Strainer

A bar or Hawthorne strainer (see right, far right) is an essential tool to prevent ice and other ingredients being poured into your glass. Some cocktails need to be double strained so even if there is a strainer in your cocktail shaker, you'll still need a separate Hawthorne strainer in your bar collection.

Juicer

A traditional, ridged half-lemon shape on a saucer will work perfectly well for juicing small amounts. There is also a citrus spout that screws into a lemon or lime and is useful for obtaining tiny amounts of juice. Mechanical or electric presses are great for large amounts of juice, but not essential in a home bar.

Other equipment

Other items you might need in your home-bar equipment are a corkscrew, bottle opener, cocktail sticks, blender, tongs, ice bucket, chopping board, knives, jugs, swizzle sticks, straws and an espuma gun for making foams.

MIXING TECHNIQUES

Shaking and stirring

These are the two most basic mixology techniques, and they are essential to master in order to confidently make a range of both classic and craft cocktails.

Shaking is when you add all the ingredients, with the specified amount of ice cubes, to the shaker and shake vigorously for approximately 5–10 seconds. The benefits of shaking are that the drink is rapidly mixed, chilled and aerated. Once the drink has been shaken, the outside of the shaker should be lightly frosted.

Shaking a cocktail will dilute your drink quite significantly. This is an essential part of the cocktail-making process and gives recipes the correct balance of taste, strength and temperature. The drink is then double-strained into glasses – the shaker should have an inbuilt strainer and you usually use a separate strainer over the glass as well. Shaking can also be used to prepare cocktails that include an ingredient that will not combine with less vigorous forms of mixing, such as an egg white.

Stirring is the purist's choice – this is a mixing technique where you add all the ingredients, usually with some ice cubes, but you combine them in a mixing glass or beaker and then stir the ingredients together using a long-handled bar spoon or swizzle stick. As with shaking, this allows you to blend and chill the ingredients without too much erosion of the ice, so you can control the level of dilution and keep it to a minimum. This simple technique is vital for drinks that do not need a lot of dilution, such as the classic Dry Martini.

Building and layering

Building is a mixology technique, explaining the task of pouring all the ingredients, one by one, usually over ice, into the serving glass. You might then stir the cocktail briefly, but this is just to mix rather than for chilling or aerating. You need to to follow built recipes exactly as the order of the ingredients can change from drink to drink and this can affect the final flavour.

Another important bartending skill is the art of layering, requiring concentration, precision and a steady hand. To make layered shooters or other drinks, you generally pour the heaviest liquid first, working through to the lightest. However, the real trick is the technique. Either touch the top of the drink with a long-handled bar spoon and pour the liquid slowly over the back of it to disperse it across the top of the ingredients already in the glass, or pour the liquid down the twisted stem that many bar spoons have. You should hold the spoon's flat disc just above the drink. Be sure to use a clean bar spoon for each layer. Floating is the term used to describe adding the top layer.

Muddling and blending

Muddling is the extraction of the juice or oils from the pulp or skin of a fruit, herb or spice. It involves mashing ingredients to release their flavours and it's usually done with a wooden pestle-like implement called a muddler.
The end that is used to crush ingredients is thicker and rounded, and the opposite, thinner end is used to stir. The best muddling technique is to keep pressing down with a twisting action until the ingredient has released all its oil or juice. If you don't have a muddler, use a pestle and mortar or the end of a wooden spoon.

As the name suggests, blending is when all the cocktail ingredients are combined in a blender or food processor. This technique is often used when mixing alcohol with fruit or with creamy ingredients that do not combine well unless they are blended. These drinks are often blended with crushed or cracked ice to produce cocktails with a smooth, frozen consistency.

Foams and airs

Foams and airs can be created in various thicknesses, from a light froth to a heavy, creamy foam. For a simple foam, use egg white, lemon juice and sugar – to top two cocktails, just whisk 1 egg white, ½ measure of lemon juice and 1 teaspoon of caster sugar together until thoroughly mixed. This mixture can then be placed into an espuma gun or cream whipper, charged, shaken and sprayed over the top of the cocktails for a light, creamy finish. The fresher the egg white, the more stable the foam, so try to use very fresh eggs.

An air is an extremely light froth with an effervescent texture that is less heavy than a foam – it can range from a bubble bath foam to the fizz on the top of a glass of champagne. To make a light air, the best ingredient to use is lecithin. Simply whisk a pinch of powdered lecithin with sugar syrup using a hand whisk or electric mixer until a light air is created. If you prefer a finer air, use a milk frother.

Chapter 1

—◇—

SIMPLE KEYS

The making of a cocktail is part of the whole gin mixology experience, but there are occasions when you want to whizz up a refreshing cocktail in an eminently smooth, no-fuss manner. Fewer ingredients help with this aspiration. Here are some ideas with a maximum of three key components, from a London French 75 to a Topaz Martini.

FROZEN G&T

Serves 1

Ingredients

crushed ice

2 measures gin

150 ml/5 fl oz tonic water

lime wedge, to garnish

1. Fill a Collins or highball glass with crushed ice.

2. Pour in the gin. Top up with tonic water. Garnish with the lime wedge and serve immediately.

VESPERS

Serves 1

Ingredients

1½ measures gin, iced

1 measure vodka, iced

½ measure dry vermouth
or Lillet

ice

lemon peel, to decorate

1. Shake the liquid ingredients over ice until frosted. Strain into a frosted martini glass. Dress with lemon peel and serve immediately.

LONDON FRENCH 75

Serves 1

Ingredients

2 measures London gin

1 measure lemon juice

cracked ice cubes

chilled champagne

1. Shake the gin and lemon juice vigorously over cracked ice until well frosted.

2. Strain into a chilled glass and top up with champagne. Serve immediately.

NAVY STRENGTH

Long voyages, stormy swells, inclement weather and the perpetual threat of enemy cannons – it is enough to make anyone reach for a strong drink. But it wasn't the extreme circumstances and sailors' thirst that led to such strong gin and other spirits being taken aboard naval ships.

Most naval vessels would store their spirits below deck in a secure part of the ship, under the watchful eye of a commanding officer. These secure caches would also hold the ship's gunpowder. This meant that higher-strength gin was required for the Navy so the gin-soaked powder would still ignite in the event of a spillage. It also ensured that the spirit had a certain level of quality and had not been watered down.

The use of gunpowder is one of the earliest methods of measuring the alcoholic strength of spirits. A few grains of gunpowder would be mixed with the spirit and ignited. If the spirit was above 57.15% ABV, the gunpowder would ignite and the spirit would be proven – this led to the term 'proof' being used as a measure of strength. It was not just the British navy that used the gunpowder method, but tax collectors and merchants, too. Any spirit synonymous with the navy usually has navy strength variations available.

GIBSON

Serves 1
Ingredients

cracked ice

3 measures gin

1 measure dry vermouth

cocktail onions, to decorate

1. Fill a cocktail glass with ice and pour over the gin and vermouth. Dress with 2–3 cocktail onions and serve immediately.

SLOE SCREW

Serves 1
Ingredients

2 measures sloe gin
orange juice
cracked ice cubes
orange slice, to decorate

1. Shake the sloe gin and orange juice over cracked ice until well frosted and pour into a chilled glass.

2. Decorate with the orange slice and serve immediately.

SILVER STREAK

Serves 1
Ingredients

ice
1 measure gin, iced
1 measure kümmel, iced

1. Fill a small old-fashioned glass or tumbler with ice and pour in the gin. Slowly pour on the kümmel and serve immediately.

ALASKA

Serves 1
Ingredients

½ measure gin
¹/₂ measure yellow Chartreuse
ice cubes

1. Shake the gin and Chartreuse over ice until well frosted.

2. Strain into a chilled glass and serve immediately.

TOPAZ MARTINI

Serves 1

Ingredients

cracked ice

2 measures gin

½ measure orange curaçao

orange peel twist, to decorate

1. Put some cracked ice into a mixing glass. Pour the gin and orange curaçao over the ice. Stir well to mix then strain into a chilled cocktail glass.

2. Dress with a twist of orange peel and serve immediately.

GREEN LADY

Serves 1
Ingredients

2 measures gin

1 measure green
Chartreuse

dash lime juice

ice

1. Shake the liquid ingredients vigorously over ice until well frosted.

2. Strain into a chilled cocktail glass and serve immediately.

RACKET CLUB

Serves 1
Ingredients

dash orange bitters

ice

1 measure gin

1 measure dry vermouth

orange peel twist, to decorate

1. Dash the orange bitters over ice in a mixing glass and pour in the gin and vermouth. Stir well to mix, then strain into a chilled cocktail glass. Dress with a twist of orange peel and serve immediately.

GLASS SLIPPER

Serves 1
Ingredients

3 measures gin

1 measure blue curaçao

ice

1. Shake the gin and curaçao over ice until well frosted. Strain into a chilled cocktail glass. Serve immediately.

FIFTY FIFTY

Serves 1
Ingredients

2 measures gin

2 measures dry vermouth

ice

cocktail olive, to decorate

1. Shake the gin and vermouth vigorously over ice until well frosted. Strain into a chilled cocktail glass, dress with an olive and serve immediately.

SEVENTH HEAVEN

Serves 1
Ingredients

2 measures gin

½ measure maraschino
liqueur

½ measure grapefruit juice

ice cubes

fresh mint sprigs,
to decorate

1. Shake all the liquid ingredients vigorously over ice until well frosted.

2. Strain into a chilled cocktail glass. Decorate with fresh mint and serve immediately.

PALM BEACH

Serves 1

Ingredients

1 measure gin

1 measure white rum

1 measure pineapple juice

cracked ice cubes

1. Shake the gin, rum and pineapple juice vigorously over ice until well frosted.

2. Strain into a chilled glass and serve immediately.

ORANGE GIN SLING

Serves 1
Ingredients

2 measures gin

4 dashes orange bitters

1. Pour the gin into a cocktail glass, then carefully splash on the orange bitters. Serve immediately.

SAKETINI

Serves 1
Ingredients

3 measures gin

½ measure sake

ice

lemon-peel twist, to decorate

1. Shake the gin and sake vigorously over ice until well frosted.

2. Strain into a chilled cocktail glass and decorate with a twist of lemon peel. Serve immediately.

Chapter 2

---◆---

CLASSIC CHORDS

Classic gin cocktails demand a sense of occasion. Think of
007's defining Vesper Martini; Gin Rickey, the refreshing,
cooling drink in *The Great Gatsby*; the Gimlet, which made
its debut in Raymond Chandler's 1950s novel *The Long
Goodbye*; and the quintessentially English Pink Gin, a
favourite in the novels of Agatha Christie and John Le Carré.

MARTINI

Serves 1

Ingredients

4–6 cracked ice cubes

3 measures gin

1 tsp dry vermouth, or to taste

cocktail olive, to decorate

1. Put the cracked ice cubes into a cocktail shaker.

2. Pour the gin and vermouth over the ice cubes.

3. Shake until well frosted. Strain into a chilled cocktail glass.

4. Decorate with the olive. Serve immediately.

NEGRONI

Serves 1
Ingredients

cracked ice

1 measure gin

1 measure Campari

½ measure sweet
vermouth

orange-peel twist, to
decorate

1. Put some ice into a mixing glass. Pour the gin, Campari and vermouth over the ice and stir well to mix.

2. Strain into a chilled glass and dress with an orange-peel twist. Serve immediately.

PINK
GIN

Serves 1
Ingredients

1 measure Plymouth Gin

few drops Angostura
bitters

1 measure water, iced

maraschino cherry, to
decorate

1. Pour the first three ingredients into a
mixing glass and stir.

2. Strain into a cocktail glass and dress with a
maraschino cherry. Serve immediately.

GIN RICKEY

Serves 1

Ingredients

cracked ice

2 measures gin

1 measure lime juice

soda water

lemon slice, to decorate

1. Fill a chilled highball glass or goblet with cracked ice.

2. Pour over the gin and lime juice.

3. Top up with soda water.

4. Stir gently to mix and decorate with a lemon slice. Serve immediately.

DUTCH COURAGE

Those suffering pre-show nerves before a performance or presentation usually welcome a strong drink. The phrase 'Dutch courage' comes from the Low Countries (modern-day Netherlands, Belgium, parts of northern France and Germany), the birthplace of genever (the grandfather of modern gin) and the Thirty Years' War of 1618–1638.

The Thirty Years' War was Europe's last major religious war centred around the Protestant reformation, and was a bloody, brutal and drawn-out affair involving several great powers in Europe. It also had lasting effects. In the early stages of the war, English soldiers were sent by Queen Elizabeth I to support Protestant forces fighting against the Catholic-led armies of the Holy Roman Empire. They stood side by side with the Dutch military and received genever to fortify themselves during battle. Troops who returned home are believed to have told tales of the 'Dutch Courage' which drove them to overcome their fears and foes on the battlefield, sowing the seeds of a love affair with juniper and gin that continues to this day.

CLOVER CLUB

Serves 1
Ingredients

2 measures gin

1 measure lime juice

1 measure grenadine

1 egg white

ice

1. Pour all ingredients over ice. Shake vigorously until well frosted. Strain into a chilled cocktail glass and serve immediately.

GIN SLING

Serves 1
Ingredients

1 sugar cube
1 measure gin
freshly grated nutmeg
lemon slice, to serve

1. Place the sugar in an old-fashioned glass and add 125 ml/4 fl oz of hot water. Stir until the sugar is dissolved.

2. Stir in the gin, sprinkle with nutmeg, and serve immediately with a slice of lemon.

SINGAPORE
SLING

Serves 1
Ingredients

cracked ice cubes

2 measures gin

1 measure cherry brandy

1 measure lemon juice

1 tsp grenadine

soda water

lime peel strips and
cocktail cherries, to
decorate

1. Put 4–6 cracked ice cubes into
a cocktail shaker and pour over
the gin.

2. Pour over the cherry brandy, lemon juice
and grenadine and shake vigorously until well
frosted.

3. Half fill a chilled glass with cracked ice
cubes and strain the cocktail over the ice.

4. Top up with soda water and decorate with
the lime peel and cherries. Serve immediately.

SMOKED
LAST WORD

Serves 1

Ingredients

¾ measure smoked gin

¾ measure lime juice

¾ measure maraschino liqueur

¾ measure green chartreuse

handful ice cubes

lime slice, to garnish

SMOKED GIN

100 g/3½ oz whisky barrel wood chips

350 ml/12 fl oz gin

1. To make the smoked gin, lay the wood chips on a metal tray and place the tray onto a heatproof, preferably metal, surface. Using a blowtorch, scorch the wood chips until roughly 50 per cent of them have blackened.

2. Place the scorched wood chips in a medium-sized, sterilized and sealable jar. Pour in the gin, and keep the gin bottle. Seal the jar and leave in a cool place for two weeks.

3. Strain the gin through a coffee filter and pour back into its bottle.

4. For the cocktail, place all the ingredients except the lime slice into a cocktail shaker. Shake well and double strain it into a coupe glass. Garnish with the lime slice and serve.

ORANGE BLOSSOM

Serves 1
Ingredients

2 measures gin

2 measures orange juice

cracked ice

orange slices, to decorate

1. Shake the gin and orange juice vigorously over ice until well frosted. Strain into a chilled cocktail glass and dress with orange slices. Serve immediately.

GIMLET

Serves 1
Ingredients

1 measure gin

½ measure fresh lime juice

ice

tonic water

lime slices, to decorate

1. Pour the gin and lime juice over ice in a chilled old-fashioned glass. Top up with tonic water and dress with slices of lime. Serve immediately.

MARTINEZ

Serves 1
Ingredients

2 measures gin, iced

1 measure Italian
vermouth

dash Angostura bitters

dash maraschino liqueur

ice

twisted lemon slice, to
decorate

1. Shake the gin, vermouth, bitters and maraschino over ice
until frosted. Strain into a chilled cocktail glass and dress
with a twisted lemon slice. Serve immediately.

LONG ISLAND ICED TEA

Serves 1

Ingredients

cracked ice

1 measure vodka

1 measure gin

1 measure white tequila

1 measure white rum

½ measure white crème de menthe

2 measures lemon juice

1 teaspoon caster sugar

cola

lime wedge, to decorate

1. Put 4–6 cracked ice cubes into a cocktail shaker. Pour all the liquid ingredients except the cola over the ice, add the sugar and shake vigorously until well frosted.

2. Half fill a tall glass with cracked ice and strain over the cocktail. Top up with cola, decorate with the lime wedge and serve immediately.

BRONX

Serves 1
Ingredients

2 measures gin

1 measure orange juice

½ measure dry vermouth

½ measure sweet vermouth

cracked ice

1. Pour the gin, orange juice, dry vermouth and sweet vermouth over ice in a mixing glass. Stir to mix and strain into a chilled cocktail glass. Serve immediately.

ALABAMA SLAMMER

Serves 1
Ingredients

1 measure Southern Comfort
1 measure Amaretto
1 measure sloe gin
cracked ice
½ tsp lemon juice

1. Pour the Southern Comfort, Amaretto and sloe gin over cracked ice in a mixing glass and stir.

2. Strain into a shot glass and add the lemon juice. Cover with your hand, slam on the table and drink immediately.

TOM COLLINS

Serves 1
Ingredients

4–6 cracked ice cubes

3 measures gin

2 measures lemon juice

½ measure sugar syrup

soda water

lemon slices, to decorate

1. Put the cracked ice cubes into a cocktail shaker.

2. Pour over the gin, lemon juice and sugar syrup and shake vigorously until well frosted.

3. Strain into a chilled Collins glass.

4. Top up with soda water and decorate with the lemon slices. Serve immediately.

MAIDEN'S PRAYER

Serves 1
Ingredients

1 measure gin

1 measure triple sec

1 tsp orange juice

1 tsp lemon juice

ice

lemon peel twist, to decorate

1. Shake the ingredients vigorously over ice until well frosted.

2. Strain into a chilled cocktail glass and decorate with the twist of lemon peel. Serve immediately.

Chapter 3

❖

CITRUS NOTES

Citrus has a strong association with cocktails – the fresh acidity of orange, lemon, lime and grapefruit typically balances out the sweeter and richer components within a cocktail. This is clearly demonstrated by the fact that gin cocktails with a zing of citrus simply cannot be restricted to the parameters of this chapter.

GIN, CHAMPAGNE & GRAPEFRUIT SORBET

Serves 6

Ingredients

200 g/7 oz golden caster sugar

100 ml/3½ fl oz water

200 ml/7 fl oz ruby grapefruit juice

6 scoops grapefruit sorbet

6 measures gin

12 splashes rhubarb bitters

1 x 750 ml/1¼ pint bottle champagne

6 grapefruit-peel twists, to garnish

1. You will need an ice-cream maker for this recipe. Gently heat the caster sugar and water in a medium-sized saucepan until the sugar has dissolved. Take off the heat and leave to cool slightly, then add the grapefruit juice.

2. Place the grapefruit mixture into an ice-cream maker and churn until frozen. Once frozen, transfer the sorbet to a plastic container and place in the freezer for a couple of hours to firm up completely.

3. When ready to serve, divide the sorbet between six cocktail glasses, followed by the gin and rhubarb bitters. Top up each glass with the champagne and garnish with the grapefruit peel. Serve immediately.

MATCHA GREEN TEA COCKTAIL

Serves 1
Ingredients

1 medium egg white

½ measure lime juice

1 tsp caster sugar

1 measure green tea and
lemon grass gin

1 measure sake

½ measure agave syrup

½ measure lime juice

ice cubes

GREEN TEA AND LEMON GRASS GIN

350 ml/12 fl oz gin

1 tsp matcha green tea
powder

2 fresh lemon grass stalks,
roughly chopped

1. The green tea and lemon grass gin takes 24 hours to infuse. To make the foam, you will need an espuma gun.

2. To make the gin, pour the gin into a medium-sized, sterilized and sealable jar. Keep the gin bottle for later use. Add the matcha green tea and lemon grass. Mix well, then seal and leave to infuse for 24 hours.

3. After 24 hours, strain the mixture through a coffee filter and pour back into the reserved gin bottle. This will keep for several months.

4. For the cocktail, lightly whisk the egg white, lime juice and sugar in a medium-sized bowl until the sugar has dissolved. Pour the egg mixture into an espuma gun and charge once.

5. Place the green tea gin, sake, agave syrup and lime juice in an ice-filled cocktail shaker. Shake vigorously until well frosted, then double-strain into an ice-filled coupe glass. Shake the espuma gun and top the cocktail with the egg-white foam. Serve immediately.

GRAPEFRUIT & CHERRY G&T

Serves 1

Ingredients

1 slice of grapefruit

4 cherries, stoned

2 measures gin

whole ice cubes

175 ml/6 fl oz tonic water

2 cherries, to decorate

1. Cut the grapefruit slice into chunks. Place the grapefruit and cherries into a cocktail shaker.

2. Using a muddler, crush the grapefruit and cherries for about 30 seconds to release the flavour and oils.

3. Add the gin to the cocktail shaker and stir. Pour the mixture into a Collins or highball glass.

4. Add some ice cubes to the glass and top up with tonic water.

5. Decorate with cherries on top and serve immediately.

STREGA
SOUR

Serves 1
Ingredients

2 measures gin

1 measure Strega

1 measure lemon juice

ice

lemon slice, to decorate

1. Shake the gin, Strega and lemon juice vigorously over ice until well frosted. Strain into a cocktail glass and dress with a slice of lemon. Serve immediately.

LEAPFROG

Serves 1

Ingredients

1 ice cube

juice of ½ lemon

2 measures gin

ginger ale

orange slice, to decorate

1. Chill a long tumbler and then add the ice, lemon juice and gin. Stir just once.

2. Top up with ginger ale to taste and dress with a slice of orange. Serve immediately.

MOTHER'S RUIN

The Gin Craze that swept through London in the early 18th century saw debauchery and depravity on an unprecedented scale. Life was hard, living conditions were appalling and the poor had very little to aspire to. Coupled with a tidal wave of cheap gin, the stage was set for a 'bender' on a monumental scale.

During this period, gin production grew dramatically. By the 1730s there was enough gin being made to support a 600,000 strong London population, supplying around 14 gallons per person per year. Gin was made using questionable methods, laced with other ingredients to mask the foul flavours emanating from the distillate. It was cheaper than beer, incredibly strong and available in every shop and filth-ridden alleyway.

By 1723 the death rate in London outweighed the birthrate. Gin became heavily identified with women and adopted one of its best-known synonyms, Mother's Ruin. The government stepped in, but its efforts failed and in some cases made the situation worse. It took until the 1760s for the city to start to sober up.

MOONLIGHT

Serves 4
Ingredients

3 measures grapefruit juice

4 measures gin

1 measure kirsch

4 measures white wine

½ tsp lemon zest

ice cubes

1. Shake all the liquid ingredients vigorously over ice until well frosted. Strain into chilled glasses and serve immediately.

GRAND ROYAL CLOVER CLUB

Serves 1

Ingredients

2 measures gin

1 measure lemon juice

1 measure grenadine

1 egg white

ice

lime-peel twist, to decorate

1. Pour the first four ingredients over ice.

2. Shake vigorously until well frosted and strain into a chilled cocktail glass.

3. Decorate with a twist of lime peel and serve immediately.

BEE'S KNEES

Serves 1
Ingredients

1 measure gin

⅓ measure fresh lemon juice

⅔ measure clear honey

ice

bitter lemon, to taste

lemon zest, to decorate

1. Shake the first three ingredients over ice until well frosted. Strain into a tall, ice-filled glass and top up with bitter lemon.

2. Dress with a few shreds of lemon zest. Serve immediately.

FIREFLY

Serves 1
Ingredients

1 measure gin

½ measure tequila

½ measure dry orange curaçao

½ measure lemon juice

dash egg white

ice

orange peel, to decorate

1. Shake all the liquid ingredients well over ice until frosted.

2. Strain into a chilled cocktail glass and decorate with a twist of orange peel. Serve immediately.

STRESSED
OUT

Serves 1
Ingredients

1 measure gin, iced

½ measure green
Chartreuse, iced

½ measure lime juice,
chilled

dash pastis, iced

sugar syrup, to taste

cubed and crushed ice

lime wedge, to decorate

1. Stir all the liquid ingredients together over ice until well frosted.

2. Strain into a small cocktail glass filled with crushed ice and add a lime wedge. Serve immediately.

BULLDOG

Serves 1

Ingredients

2 measures gin

1 measure fresh orange juice

ice

ginger ale

orange slice

1. Stir the gin and orange juice over ice in a medium tumbler. Top up with ginger ale and add a slice of orange. Serve immediately.

BRIDE'S MOTHER

Serves 1
Ingredients

1½ measures sloe gin

1 measure gin

2½ measures grapefruit juice

½ measure sugar syrup

ice cubes and crushed ice

grapefruit slices, to decorate

1. Shake the liquid ingredients vigorously over ice cubes until well frosted.

2. Strain over crushed ice and decorate with grapefruit slices. Serve immediately.

FALLEN ANGEL

Serves 1
Ingredients

1 dash Angostura bitters

juice of 1 lemon or lime

2 measures gin

ice

green crème de menthe

1. Shake the first three ingredients over ice and strain into a cocktail glass. Top with two dashes of crème de menthe at the last minute. Serve immediately.

SLOE KISS

Serves 1
Ingredients

4–6 cracked ice cubes

½ measure sloe gin

½ measure Southern Comfort

1 measure vodka

1 tsp Amaretto

splash Galliano

orange juice

orange peel twist, to decorate

1. Put the cracked ice cubes into a cocktail shaker, pour over the sloe gin, Southern Comfort, vodka and Amaretto and shake until well frosted.

2. Strain into a long, chilled glass filled with cracked ice. Splash on the Galliano.

3. Top up with orange juice and decorate with the orange peel. Serve immediately.

HAWAIIAN ORANGE BLOSSOM

Serves 1
Ingredients

2 measures gin

1 measure triple sec

2 measures orange juice

1 measure pineapple juice

ice

pineapple slices and leaves,
to decorate

1. Shake the liquid ingredients vigorously over ice until well frosted.

2. Strain into a chilled wine glass and serve immediately decorated with pineapple slices and leaves.

Chapter 4

❖

EXOTIC RHYTHMS

Glamorous, magical, bizarre, enticing – escape the everyday,
search for something different and enter a wonder-world of
cocktail enchantment. Here you'll find cherries, pineapple
and pomegranate; coconut, cream and yogurt; and Frangelico,
blackberry brandy and maraschino. Break down the barriers
and be seduced by the otherworldly.

GREEK YOGURT COCKTAIL

Serves 1

Ingredients

2 measures gin

1 measure Frangelico

1 tbsp Greek-style yogurt

1 measure agave syrup

½ ripe nectarine, stoned

1 measure lemon juice

crushed ice

nectarine slice, to garnish

1. Place the gin, Frangelico, yogurt, agave syrup, nectarine and lemon juice in a cocktail shaker.

2. Using a cocktail muddler, crush all the ingredients to a smooth pulp.

3. Fill a Collins or highball glass with crushed ice. Strain the cocktail over the ice.

4. Garnish with the nectarine slice and serve immediately.

GIN & COCONUT COCKTAIL

Serves 4

Ingredients

10 g/¼ oz coconut flesh, finely grated

4 measures gin

4 measures bourbon

2 measures agave syrup

4 measures lime juice

600 ml/1 pint coconut water

4 handfuls ice cubes

4 lime slices, to garnish

1. In a small, dry frying pan, gently toast the coconut until golden. Take off the heat and leave to cool.

2. Grind the cooled coconut in a spice grinder until it becomes a fine powder. Set aside.

3. Place the gin, bourbon, agave syrup, lime juice and coconut water in a large jug and mix well.

4. Divide the gin mixture between four ice-filled Collins or highball glasses.

5. Garnish each cocktail with a teaspoon of coconut powder and the lime slices. Serve immediately.

GIN, CHERRY & APPLE SLUSHIE

Serves 4

Ingredients

150 g/5½ oz fresh cherries, stoned

1 measure lemon juice

50 g/1¾ oz golden caster sugar

8 measures gin

600 ml/1 pint apple juice

4 handfuls ice cubes

1. Place the cherries, lemon juice and sugar in a medium-sized saucepan. Gently heat until the sugar has dissolved and the cherries have broken down. Take off the heat and leave to cool for 5 minutes.

2. Once cooled, transfer the cherry mixture to a blender and blend until smooth. Push it through a fine sieve to make a purée.

3. Place the gin, cherry purée, apple juice and ice in the blender and blend until smooth.

4. Divide the slushie between four glasses and serve immediately.

HARLEM

Serves 1

Ingredients

2 measures gin

1½ measures pineapple
juice

1 tsp maraschino liqueur

1 tbsp chopped fresh
pineapple

ice

lime leaf, to decorate

1. Shake the first four ingredients vigorously
over ice until well frosted.

2. Strain into a small chilled tumbler and
dress with a lime leaf. Serve immediately.

MAGNOLIA BLOSSOM

Serves 1

Ingredients

2 measures gin

1 measure lemon juice

1 measure single cream

ice

1. Shake the ingredients vigorously over ice until well frosted.

2. Strain into a chilled cocktail glass and serve immediately.

SHAKEN, NOT STIRRED...

It's no secret that many of the world's greatest leaders, artists, musicians and writers have been known to enjoy a gin or two. One of the most famous figures associated with gin is, of course, Ian Fleming's James Bond. Bond's taste for a martini has become legendary, and has resulted in the classic line being the bane of many mixologists' careers.

The gin trail continues with J.K. Rowling's liking for G&T; F. Scott Fitzgerald, who had a soft spot for a Gin Rickey; Raymond Chandler, who favoured a Gimlet; and Queen Elizabeth II, who is partial to a Gin and Dubonnet. So gin is woven into our history and culture.

Aside from the world of 007, martini is actually better stirred rather than shaken. This is to avoid 'bruising' the gin, to avoid overdiluting the drink and to preserve the 'mouthfeel' of the ingredients. The martini is in fact a wickedly strong cocktail, which traditionally contains a hefty amount of gin. It is the best drink to aid in an assassination – and one to assassinate your evening if you have too many! But, let's face it, if you held a 'licence to kill' and were on the case of a maniacal villain, you would probably be after a stiff drink too...

GOLDEN DAWN

Serves 1

Ingredients

½ measure gin

½ measure Calvados

½ measure apricot brandy

½ measure mango juice

ice

dash grenadine

1. Mix the first four ingredients together over ice.

2. Strain into a cocktail glass and gradually add a dash grenadine so the colour ripples through. Serve immediately.

TEARDROP

Serves 1

Ingredients

1 measure gin

2 measures apricot nectar
or peach nectar

1 measure single cream

crushed ice

½ measure strawberry
syrup

fresh strawberry and peach
slices, to decorate

1. Put the gin, apricot nectar and cream into a blender and blend for 5–10 seconds until thick and frothy.

2. Pour into a long glass that has been filled with crushed ice.

3. Splash the strawberry syrup on the top and decorate with the strawberry and peach slices. Serve immediately.

TURKISH DELIGHT GIN COCKTAIL

Serves 1

Ingredients

2 measures gin

175 ml/6 fl oz cranberry juice

1 tbsp honey

¼ tsp rosewater

a few ice cubes

1 tbsp pomegranate seeds

¼ tsp dried rose petals, plus extra to decorate

1. Pour the gin, cranberry juice, honey and rosewater into a Collins or highball glass.

2. Stir with a bar spoon until the honey has dissolved.

3. Add the ice cubes, pomegranate seeds and rose petals, then stir again.

4. Decorate with the rose petals and serve immediately with a straw.

POLISH SIDECAR

Serves 1
Ingredients

2 measures gin

1 measure blackberry
brandy

1 measure lemon juice

ice

1. Pour the gin, blackberry brandy and lemon juice over ice
and shake vigorously until well frosted, then strain into a
chilled cocktail glass. Serve immediately.

BLUE TRAIN

Serves 1
Ingredients

2 measures gin

1 measure triple sec

1 measure lemon juice

splash blue curaçao

cracked ice

1. Pour all of the ingredients into a cocktail shaker filled with ice.

2. Shake vigorously until frosted and strain into a chilled cocktail glass. Serve immediately.

WEDDING BELLE

Serves 1
Ingredients

2 measures gin

2 measures Dubonnet

1 measure cherry brandy

1 measure orange juice

ice cubes

orange-peel twist,
to decorate

1. Shake the liquid ingredients over ice until well frosted.

2. Strain into a chilled glass and garnish with a twist of orange peel. Serve immediately.

BLUE BLOODED

Serves 1
Ingredients

1 measure gin

1 measure passion-fruit nectar

4 cubes melon or mango

cracked ice

1–2 tsp blue curaçao

1. Put the gin, passion-fruit nectar, melon cubes and 4–6 cracked ice cubes into a blender and blend until smooth and frosted.

2. Pour into a tall, chilled glass filled with cracked ice and top with the curaçao. Serve immediately.

ALEXANDER

Serves 1

Ingredients

1 measure gin

1 measure crème de cacao

1 measure single cream

cracked ice

freshly grated nutmeg,
to decorate

1. Shake the first three ingredients vigorously over ice until well frosted.

2. Strain into a chilled cocktail glass and dress with grated nutmeg. Serve immediately.

FRUIT CRAZY

Serves 1
Ingredients

1 measure gin
½ measure melon liqueur
1 measure mango nectar
1 measure grapefruit juice
1 small egg white
ice cubes
mango slice, to decorate

1. Shake the first five ingredients together over ice until frosted.

2. Strain into a chilled long glass with more ice to fill, and dress with a slice of mango. Serve immediately.

PUSSYCAT

Serves 1
Ingredients

cracked ice
dash grenadine
2 measures gin
pineapple juice
pineapple slice, to decorate

_1._ Half fill a chilled tumbler with cracked ice.

_2._ Dash the grenadine over the ice and add the gin.

_3._ Top up with pineapple juice and decorate with the pineapple slice. Serve immediately.

BLOODHOUND

Serves 1
Ingredients

2 measures gin

1 measure sweet vermouth

1 measure dry vermouth

3 strawberries, plus one to decorate

4–6 cracked ice cubes

1. Put the gin, sweet vermouth, dry vermouth and strawberries into a blender.

2. Add the cracked ice. Blend until smooth.

3. Pour into a chilled cocktail glass and decorate with the remaining strawberry. Serve immediately.

Chapter 5

---◈---

HEADY BEATS

Ready for a pulsating experience? It's time to be
transported by the splendour of a convivial cocktail.
From Mango & Black Pepper Cocktail and Rolls-Royce 2
to Spiced Whiskey Sour and Old Etonian, and featuring
everything from dark rum and Grand Marnier to crème de
noyaux, prepare yourself for a heady ride.

MANGO & BLACK PEPPER COCKTAIL

Serves 1

Ingredients

1 measure gin

1 measure dark rum

1 tsp soft brown sugar

1 measure lime juice

100 ml/3½ fl oz pineapple juice

ice cubes

soda water

mango slice, to garnish

freshly ground black pepper, to garnish

1. Place the gin, rum, brown sugar, lime juice and pineapple juice in a cocktail shaker.

2. Fill the cocktail shaker with ice and shake until the mixture is well frosted.

3. Strain into an ice-filled Collins or highball glass.

4. Top up with soda water and garnish with the mango slice and a grinding of black pepper. Serve immediately.

POMEGRANATE & MINT SHRUB

Serves 1

Ingredients

crushed ice

1 measure gin

1 measure Grand Marnier

sprig of mint, to decorate

1 tsp pomegranate seeds, to decorate

POMEGRANATE SYRUP

200 g/7 oz pomegranate seeds

400 g/14 oz caster sugar

20 mint leaves

500 ml/17 fl oz raw cider vinegar

1. This cocktail takes 2 days to infuse. In a medium bowl, muddle the pomegranate seeds, sugar and mint until the seeds are crushed. Cover and leave in the refrigerator to macerate for 24 hours. Remove from the refrigerator and stir in the vinegar. Cover again and leave for another 24 hours.

2. Strain the mixture through a muslin. Pour into a sterilized, sealable jar.

3. Fill a highball glass with crushed ice. Add 2 measures of the pomegranate syrup to the glass. The rest can be stored in the refrigerator for up to 2 months.

4. Add the gin and Grand Marnier to the glass and stir with a bar spoon. Decorate with the mint and pomegranate and serve.

CHILLI G&T

Serves 1

Ingredients

handful ice cubes

2 measures
chilli-infused gin

3 splashes molasses bitters

150 ml/5 fl oz tonic water

lime slice, to garnish

CHILLI-INFUSED GIN

1 dried pasilla chilli

350 ml/12 fl oz gin

1. To make the chilli-infused gin, split the chilli in half and place it in the gin bottle. Leave to infuse for one week.

2. To make the cocktail, fill a Collins or highball glass with ice.

3. Add the gin and molasses bitters and top up with tonic water.

4. Garnish with the lime slice and serve immediately.

SPICED WHISKEY SOUR

Serves 1

Ingredients

1 measure gin

1 measure Pedro Ximénez sherry

1 measure bourbon

1 measure lemon juice

1 measure spiced syrup

1 medium egg white

handful ice cubes

SPICED SYRUP

½ cinnamon stick

2 star anise

6 black peppercorns

330 g/11½ oz caster sugar

150 ml/5 fl oz water

¾ measure vodka

1. To make the spiced syrup, gently heat all the ingredients in a medium-sized saucepan over a low heat until all the sugar has dissolved.

2. Take off the heat and leave to cool, then strain and pour into a bottle. The syrup will keep in the fridge for up to six months.

3. To make the cocktail, place the gin, sherry, bourbon, lemon juice, spiced syrup and egg white in a cocktail shaker. Dry-shake all the ingredients. Add the ice and shake vigorously for 30 seconds to create a foam.

4. Double-strain into a lowball glass and serve immediately.

ROAD RUNNER

Serves 1
Ingredients

2 measures gin
½ measure dry vermouth
½ measure Pernod
1 tsp grenadine
cracked ice

1. Shake the gin, vermouth, Pernod and grenadine vigorously over ice until well frosted. Strain into a chilled wine glass and serve immediately.

BELLINI MARTINI

Serves 1
Ingredients

1 measure gin

½ measure brandy

½ measure peach purée

splash of sweet vermouth

ice

peach slice, to decorate

1. Shake the first four ingredients over ice until well frosted. Strain into an iced martini glass and dress with a slice of peach. Serve immediately.

INCA

Serves 1
Ingredients

1 measure gin

1 measure sweet vermouth

1 measure dry sherry

dash orgeat syrup

dash orange bitters

1. Pour all the ingredients into a glass and stir. This is one that does not need to be chilled. Serve immediately.

BACHELOR'S BAIT

***Serves* 1**
Ingredients

2 measures gin
1 tsp grenadine
1 egg white
ice
dash orange bitters

1. Shake the gin, grenadine and egg white together over ice cubes until well frosted.

2. Add the orange bitters, give the mixture another quick shake and strain into a chilled cocktail glass. Serve immediately.

OLD ETONIAN

Serves 1
Ingredients

cracked ice

dash crème de noyaux

dash orange bitters

1 measure gin

1 measure Lillet blanc

1. Put some ice into a mixing glass and add the liquid ingredients.

2. Stir to mix well, then strain into a chilled cocktail glass. Serve immediately.

MODERN GIN

❖

Over the last decade, gin has risen to become one of the leading spirits in the UK and the US. Its seemingly unstoppable rise in popularity has been mirrored in the release of hundreds of gin brands and a plethora of specialist bars appearing in cities the world over.

From its somewhat debauched origins in the slums of London, gin has climbed the ladder to reach the peak of sophistication. A true underdog of the spirits world and a classic rags-to-riches tale, this is a feat worthy of recognition. Dozens of factors have combined over the last decade to create this sudden renaissance. Most notably the micro-distilling boom has led to a fresh wave of artisan distillers creating gins with different flavours, and a soaring global thirst for cocktails has been driven by younger generations looking for drinks with flavour and provenance.

However you choose to buy and drink your gin, you are undoubtedly playing a part in another chapter of gin's history. The gin boom of the early 21st century is certainly one that will not be forgotten.

KARINA

Serves 1

Ingredients

1 measure gin

½ measure Dubonnet

½ measure mandarin
liqueur

juice of ½ lemon

ice

1. Mix the ingredients together in a large tumbler filled with ice and stir until the glass is frosted. Serve immediately.

JOCKEY CLUB SPECIAL

Serves 1

Ingredients

1 measure gin

½ measure crème de noyaux

good splash lemon juice

2 dashes orange bitters

2 dashes Angostura bitters

ice

lemon wedge, to decorate

1. Stir the ingredients well over ice and strain into a cocktail glass. Dress with a lemon wedge. Serve immediately.

ROLLS-ROYCE 2

Serves 1

Ingredients

ice

3 measures gin

1 measure dry vermouth

1 measure sweet vermouth

¼ tsp Benedictine

1. Put 4–6 ice cubes into a mixing glass. Pour the ingredients over the ice. Stir well to mix, then strain into a chilled cocktail glass. Serve immediately.

GREAT DANE

Serves 1

Ingredients

2 measures gin

1 measure cherry brandy

½ measure dry vermouth

1 tsp kirsch

ice

lemon peel, to decorate

1. Shake the gin, cherry brandy, vermouth and kirsch vigorously over ice until well frosted. Strain into a chilled cocktail glass. Dress with lemon peel. Serve immediately.

STAR WARS

Serves 1
Ingredients

2 measures gin

2 measures lemon juice

1 measure Galliano

1 measure crème de noyaux

ice

lemon-peel twist, to
decorate

1. Shake the first four ingredients vigorously over ice until
well frosted. Strain into a chilled cocktail glass and dress with
a twist of lemon peel. Serve immediately.

MISSISSIPPI MULE

Serves 1
Ingredients

2 measures gin

½ measure cassis

½ measure lemon juice

cubed and crushed ice

1. Shake the ingredients vigorously over ice until well frosted. Strain over crushed ice into a small chilled tumbler. Serve immediately.

Chapter 6

---◆---

SPARKLING CUTS

If you like to have a fizz in your tail – or rather in your cocktail – look no further. To make these cocktails effervesce we have prosecco, cider, soda and champagne. Each one is partnered with ingredients in magical combinations to ensure that your drink, your companions and your time together are vibrant and sparkling.

GIN SWIZZLE

Serves 1

Ingredients

100 g/3½ oz whisky-barrel woodchips

350 ml/12 fl oz gin

1 measure lime juice

2 tsp caster sugar

1 tsp Angostura bitters

large handful of crushed ice

175 ml/6 fl oz soda water

lime slice, to decorate

1. This cocktail takes 2 weeks to infuse and you need a blowtorch. Lay the woodchips on a metal tray and place onto a heatproof surface.

2. Scorch all over the woodchips with a blowtorch until about half have blackened. Put the scorched woodchips into a sterilized, sealable jar, then pour in the gin. Keep the gin bottle. Mix and seal the jar. Leave in a cool place for 2 weeks.

3. Strain the gin through a fine sieve. Place 2 measures of smoked gin, the lime juice, caster sugar and bitters into a highball glass. The rest of the gin can be stored for up to 2 months. Add the ice to the glass and top up with the soda water. Froth well with a swizzle stick and serve immediately with a lime slice.

HONEY & LEMON PROSECCO

Serves 1

Ingredients

1 measure gin

¼ measure honey

¼ measure lemon juice

85 ml/3 fl oz chilled prosecco

1. Mix the gin, honey and lemon juice in a small jug.

2. Pour the mixture into a chilled coupe glass.

3. Top up with the chilled prosecco. Serve immediately.

ELDERFLOWER & MARASCHINO CLUB SODA

Serves 1

Ingredients

handful ice cubes

1 measure gin

1 measure elderflower liqueur

1 measure maraschino liqueur

½ measure lemon juice

150 ml/5 fl oz club soda

lemon wedge, to garnish (optional)

maraschino cherry, to garnish

1. Fill a Collins or highball glass with ice cubes.

2. Add the gin, elderflower liqueur, maraschino liqueur and lemon juice.

3. Stir the mixture with a cocktail stirrer.

4. Top up with the club soda.

5. Garnish with the lemon wedge, if using, and cherry. Serve immediately.

LIME & LEMON GRASS SLING

Serves 1

Ingredients

½ lime

1 small lemon grass stick, trimmed

2 measures gin

½ measure Benedictine

½ measure cherry brandy liqueur

2 dashes orange bitters

whole ice cubes

150 ml/5 fl oz soda water

lemon slice and fresh cherry, to decorate

1. Cut the lime into wedges and then slice the lemon grass thinly.

2. Place the lime and lemon grass into a cocktail shaker.

3. Using a muddler, crush the lime and the lemon grass to release the juice and oils.

4. Add the gin, Benedictine, cherry brandy and orange bitters to the cocktail shaker.

5. Pour the mixture into a sling or highball glass. Add some ice cubes and top up with soda water. Decorate with the lemon slice and cherry and serve immediately.

NEW ORLEANS GIN FIZZ

Serves 1

Ingredients

juice of ½ lemon

2 tsp icing sugar

1 small egg white

2 measures gin

2 dashes orange flower
water

1 tbsp single cream

ice

soda water

orange peel and a flower,
to decorate

1. Shake the first six ingredients over ice until
well frosted. Strain into a chilled tall tumbler
and top up with soda water to taste.

2. Dress with a shred of orange peel and
a flower. Serve immediately.

LONDONER

Serves 1

Ingredients

2 measures London dry gin

½ measure fraise, rosehip
or any fruit syrup

2 measures lemon juice

½ measure dry vermouth

ice

soda water

lemon peel twist, to
decorate

1. Mix the first four ingredients over ice in a highball glass or large tumbler. Top up with soda water and dress with a twist of lemon peel. Serve immediately.

MEDICINAL GIN

Juniperus communis, also known as Juniper, is part of the cypress family of plants and is thought to have first appeared during the Triassic period, 250 million years ago. Juniper can be found on almost every continent, weather permitting, and has been used by man to treat numerous ailments for thousands of years.

Its medicinal properties were exploited by most ancient civilisations, including those of the Egyptians, Greeks and Arabs. Its use continued into the Middle Ages, treating everything from toothaches to tapeworms. It was even used as a contraceptive and to induce abortion. Typically the plant was imbibed in a concoction of wine, spices and herbs.

No one knows with certainty how juniper first made contact with distilled spirits, but the earliest references of juniper-flavoured spirits date back to the mid-1500s. What we do know is it was the Dutch who created the very first 'Genevers', the forerunners to English and modern gin. Today we know that imbibing alcohol and juniper are not conducive to curing illness or preventing pregnancy. However, depending on your circumstance, the ancient healing properties of juniper might make for a reasonable excuse to crack open the gin.

APPLE CLASSIC

Serves 1
Ingredients

½ measure gin

½ measure brandy

½ measure Calvados

ice

sweet cider

apple slice, to decorate

1. Shake the gin, brandy and Calvados over ice until frosted.

2. Strain into a glass and top up with cider to taste. Dress with a slice of apple. Serve immediately.

BELLE COLLINS

Serves 1
Ingredients

2 fresh mint sprigs, plus extra to decorate

2 measures gin

1 measure lemon juice

1 tsp sugar syrup

4–6 crushed ice cubes

sparkling water

1. Muddle the mint sprigs.

2. Place the mint in a chilled tumbler and pour in the gin, lemon juice and sugar syrup. Add the crushed ice cubes to the glass.

3. Top up with sparkling water, stir gently and decorate with more fresh mint. Serve immediately.

SOUTHERN FIZZ

Serves 1

Ingredients

2 measures gin

1 measure fresh lime juice

1 measure passion fruit
juice

¼ measure sugar syrup

3 dashes orange flower
water

1 measure soda water

crushed ice

1. Mix all the ingredients together in a blender on fast for a few seconds or until really frothy.

2. Pour into a large iced cocktail glass or highball glass and serve immediately.

DAISY

Serves 1
Ingredients

4–6 cracked ice cubes

3 measures gin

1 measure lemon juice

1 tbsp grenadine

1 tsp sugar syrup

soda water

orange wedge, to decorate

1. Put the cracked ice cubes into a cocktail shaker.

2. Pour over the gin, lemon juice, grenadine and sugar syrup and shake vigorously until well frosted.

3. Strain the cocktail into a chilled highball glass. Top up with soda water, stir gently and decorate with the orange wedge. Serve immediately.

STAR DAISY

Serves 1
Ingredients

2 measures gin

1½ measures apple brandy

1½ measures lemon juice

1 tsp sugar syrup

½ tsp triple sec

crushed ice

soda water

1. Pour the first five ingredients over ice and shake vigorously until well frosted. Strain into a tumbler half filled with ice, then top up with soda water. Serve immediately.

MONTE CARLO

Serves 1
Ingredients

4–6 ice cubes

½ measure gin

¼ measure lemon juice

champagne or sparkling
white wine, chilled

¼ measure crème de
menthe

fresh mint sprig, to
decorate

1. Put the ice into a mixing glass, pour over the gin and lemon juice. Stir until well chilled.

2. Strain into a chilled champagne flute and top up with champagne.

3. Drizzle the crème de menthe over the top and decorate with the mint sprig. Serve immediately.

SLOE GIN RICKEY

Serves 1
Ingredients

cracked ice

2 measures sloe gin

1 measure lime juice

soda water

lime slice

1. Fill a chilled highball glass or goblet with ice. Pour the gin and lime juice over the ice. Top up with soda water. Stir gently to mix and dress with a lime slice. Serve immediately.

END OF THE ROAD

Serves 1

Ingredients

3 measures gin

1 measure crème de menthe

1 measure pastis

ice

100 ml/3½ fl oz soda water

fresh mint sprig, to decorate

1. Stir the first three ingredients over ice. Strain into a tall glass filled with ice, top up with the soda water and dress with a sprig of mint. Serve immediately.

ALICE SPRINGS

Serves 1

Ingredients

3 measures gin

½ tsp grenadine

1 measure orange juice

1 measure lemon juice

ice

soda water

3 drops Angostura bitters

1. Shake the first four ingredients together over ice until frosted.

2. Strain into a chilled tall glass and top up with soda water. Sprinkle in the Angostura bitters.

GIN SANGAREE

Serves 1
Ingredients

cracked ice

2 measures gin

½ tsp sugar syrup

sparkling water

1 tbsp port

freshly grated nutmeg,
for sprinkling

1. Put some ice into a chilled tumbler. Pour the gin and sugar syrup over the ice, then top up with sparkling water. Stir gently to mix, then float the port on top.

2. Sprinkle with freshly grated nutmeg and serve immediately.

BLEU BLEU BLEU

Serves 1
Ingredients

crushed ice
1 measure gin
1 measure vodka
1 measure tequila
1 measure fresh lemon juice
2 dashes egg white
1 measure blue curaçao
soda water
lemon slice, to decorate

1. Put 4–6 crushed ice cubes into a cocktail shaker.

2. Add the gin, vodka, tequila, lemon juice, egg white and curaçao and shake until frosted.

3. Strain the cocktail into a tall glass filled with crushed ice and top up with soda water. Decorate with a lemon slice. Serve immediately.

INDEX

This edition published by Parragon Books Ltd in 2017

LOVE FOOD is an imprint of Parragon Books Ltd

Parragon Books Ltd
Chartist House
15–17 Trim Street
Bath BA1 1HA, UK
www.parragon.com/lovefood

ISBN 978-1-4748-7094-8

Printed in China

Introduction: Joe Clark
New recipes: Lincoln Jefferson
New photography: Mike Cooper
Home economy: Lincoln Jefferson
Cover design: Lexi L'Esteve

Notes for the Reader

This book uses both metric and imperial measurements. Follow the same units of measurement throughout; do not mix metric and imperial. All spoon measurements are level: teaspoons are assumed to be 5 ml, and tablespoons are assumed to be 15 ml.
One measure is assumed to be 25 ml/¾ fl oz. Unless otherwise stated, milk is assumed to be full fat, eggs and individual fruits and vegetables are medium, pepper is freshly ground black pepper and salt is table salt. A pinch of salt is calculated as $\frac{1}{16}$ of a teaspoon.
Unless otherwise stated, all root vegetables should be peeled prior to using.

Please consume alcohol responsibly.